Once you start reading it you will find it hard to put down. It will draw you in because the stories are so relatable to your own life. This book is reality on steroids. I love every page of this powerful book about life. You will want to read it and share it with your mother, daughter, sister, and girlfriend. ~ **Patricia Ashley, Conference Speaker, Teacher, Author, Marriage God's Way**

This collection of vignettes and poignant commentary will remind believers that we are not the first to face challenges in life, neither are we helpless in our struggles. Through stories that ring true-to-life and references to our best source of wisdom—the Word of God—the authors bring us into the kinds of conversations we need to have with one another and with Him. ~ **Michelle Stimpson, Bestselling Author, Speaker & Teacher**

Coveted Conversations is a delightful and easy-to-read treasure of God's wisdom for women by women. A practical guide to share Godly advice about everyday struggles. This book offers suggestions about relationships with an intimate look at relatable situations in a clear and concise manner. It is one of the most practical, insightful books I have ever read! If women have a desire to get real answers then don't just have a conversation, reach for a Coveted Conversation! ~ **Juanita Budd, Speaker, Executive Director of Austin Free-Net**

COVETED CONVERSATIONS

AUTHENTIC STORIES THAT INSPIRE WOMEN TO

GROW AND LIVE INTENTIONALLY

SHAILENDRA THOMAS   MARILYN RANDLE

JENNIFER SMITH

Edifying Reads by MLStimpson Enterprises

9/29/18
Dear Yvonne,
I am so glad that God saw to fit for us to work together on this team. I truly enjoyed visiting with you. I have to know you - personally & professionally these past 3 days. I will be praying for you and your husband. I hope you enjoy the book!

Finish Well!
Acts 20:24

Fondly!
Shailendra Thomas

All scripture notations are taken from the NEW INTERNATIONAL VERSION (NIV): Scripture taken from THE HOLY BIBLE, NEW INTERNATIONAL VERSION ®. Copyright© 1973, 1978, 1984, 2011 by Biblica, Inc.™. Used by permission of Zondervan.

Published by Edifying Reads, MLStimpson Enterprises
P.O. Box 1592
Cedar Hill, TX 75106
ISBN 1-943563-11-X
Library of Congress PCN: 2017954231

Cover design by Paul Ernest
Cover and author photography by King Harrell
Editing by Trisha Heddlesten

DEDICATION

This book is dedicated to our precious mothers,
Sandra Jean, Willie Mae, and Clarice Olita,
who were always available for a
Coveted Conversation.

TABLE OF CONTENTS

Salty

ACKNOWLEDGMENTS

Special thanks to our husbands,
Richard, Gary, and Doug,
for giving us the time, freedom,
and encouragement to write.
...I found the one my heart loves. – Song of Solomon 3:4a

We would also like to express our sincere appreciation to
Michelle Stimpson (publisher), Paul Ernest (cover concept
and design), King Harrell (cover & author photography),
and Trisha Heddlesten (editor). The completion of this
book could not have been possible without their
contributions, assistance, and participation.

FOREWORD

I have had the privilege of knowing the authors of *Coveted Conversations* for over 25 years. They are women whose godly integrity has always been consistent. They each possess the qualities of being honest and having strong godly convictions. They live lives of great moral character. They are women who have committed themselves to Jesus, their family, church/ministries, and their community. They each have a compassion to help people and to relieve suffering.

I have personally been the recipient of their hospitality, prayers, support and godly wisdom. One of the authors and her husband opened their home to my husband and I while we were in transition. Before they left for an out-of-town trip, they gave us the keys to their beautiful home to stay in and relax. When we arrived we were delightfully surprised as the author had prepared an amazing meal for us. The author's mother had baked a German chocolate cake from scratch and it was wonderful!

Their hospitality was so selfless.

I have witnessed these women making whatever sacrifices necessary to honor God in their lives. It speaks to their credibility for the conversations found in the pages of this book. For such a time as this, God will use the conversations in this book to speak to the hearts of his people.

The Bible says to guard the heart with all diligence, for out of it are the issues of life. (Proverbs 4:23) In order to guard the heart, we must be intentional. It is imperative that we develop Biblical belief systems in our hearts. We must hide the Word in our hearts (memorize it) so that we will be able to counter wrong thinking and the temptations that come in the form of deceptive messages from the world and Satan.

Our belief system needs reprogramming because our hearts in its natural state only produces evil thoughts. (Matthew 15:19, Proverbs 23:7) Changing our belief system is the only way for us to truly be transformed in what we think, say and do. We must engraft the Word of God in order to produce right thinking, right choices and right living. Thy word have I hid in my heart, that I might not sin against thee. (Psalm 119:11)

Building a belief system is not an intellectual exercise, but a heart examination. Our belief system controls and determines our destiny. Your belief system is the integration of your desires, convictions, and commitments of your heart. It is where you experience fulfillment and fruitfulness. If your system is faulty, then you will experience frustration and disillusion. God promises to give us the desires (belief system) of our hearts if we delight in Him. (Psalm 37:4) Remember Jeremiah 17:10, God is the one who searches the heart and rewards you according to your ways and actions. As you listen to each conversation in this book, you will hear sound Biblical counsel.

Reading this book is equal to sitting in a warm, comfortable, safe environment and having an intimate conversation with honest, godly, and wise friends who are willing to share their life experiences. They are transparent as they share their stories. They keep it real while giving you godly counsel and hope. In this book, they will address the many life issues that we, as women, are confronted with.

You will read about how to recover from loss and wrong choices of your past, and also how to forgive yourself and move on with your life. You will read about heartwarming relationships that encourage and establish legacy in the lives of children. You will receive encouragement as a single woman and how to be content in the season that you are in. If you're grieving the loss of a loved one you can experience healing as the authors share how God met them in their season of grief. These ladies even address Church hurt and how to remain faithful.

Each story is short and powerful with Biblical

solutions. You will be given an opportunity to examine your own heart and life. They have put it out there and dealt with the topics that are not often addressed. Their stories will motivate, inspire, encourage, instruct, and transform your life.

Once you start reading it you will find it hard to put it down. It will draw you in because the stories are so relatable to your own life. This book is reality on steroids. I love every page of this powerful book about life. You will want to read it and share it with your mother, daughter, sister and girlfriend.

Pat Ashley
Conference Speaker/Teacher
Author, *Marriage is a Blessing*

INTRODUCTION

Have you ever wanted to share an intimate story? Do you know the feeling of eagerly anticipating that special conversation with a close friend, your mom, dear sister, or special aunt? The following is a collection of stories that can be enjoyed alone or shared with someone close. Some are sad, some are stirring, some are humorous; all are inspiring.

The stories are divided into sections that speak to the "flavor" of each selection. An inspirational segment after each story has been included for those who want to reflect and apply practical revelations gleaned.

So grab your favorite drink, find a cozy corner, and experience a *Coveted Conversation*.

SAVORY

Full of Flavor Conversations

CRYING OVER SPILT MILK

I am the product of suburban middle class America. My father was a great businessman, provider, and leader for our family. My mother was intelligent, beautiful, loving, and nurturing. My family went to church every Sunday and actually practiced what was preached. I accepted Christ at an early age and attended children's church, youth service, and Christian camps. We sat down to dinner every night as a family, and took family vacations in the summer.

My family and church relationships were rich and meaningful, and I felt loved and valued. So why did I feel the need to look for affection and affirmation elsewhere? Why was I so intoxicated by the attention and flattery of a boy that I would make a choice I would regret for the rest of my life? I met Robert at a 4th of July party at the beach. He was a friend of a friend of a friend. I don't even know why I was attracted to this average-looking guy. But when we were introduced, he was so warm and inviting, and looked at me as though he knew me. We had an immediate connection. As we spoke, he validated me in so many ways. He was impressed by my career, complimentary of my education, and in awe of my appearance. His praise was alluring, despite the fact that my parents had always affirmed me.

After a couple of dates, I knew I should have called it quits, but I enjoyed having someone so interested in me. I knew he was struggling financially, but I thought that he was just between jobs. I knew he was moody, but he was so cute when he pouted. I knew he was not very spiritual, but he did attend church service with me every now and then. How did I overlook that, at 27 years of age, Robert did not have a job, car, or an address?

As a teenager, my mother made sure that I read every "True Love Waits" resource available and my father even presented me with a purity ring at a special ceremony where I pledged that I would abstain from sex until marriage. But Robert was different. And even though we had some bumps in our relationship, it did not take long before I knew he was the one for me. When we united physically, I felt guilty at first, but my guilt was quickly quenched by the thought of spending the rest of my life with Robert. Mom and Dad had several concerns about our future, but I did not care or listen. I have no excuses.

The first few months of our marriage, I felt like we were living my dream. But after a year, I started wondering why Robert could not keep a job. My salary as a graphic designer was barely paying the rent, food, and utilities. If we were ever going to purchase a home, travel, or have children, he would have to find stable employment.

One evening, after sharing my concerns with him regarding our finances, he exploded and did not speak or touch me physically for weeks. I quickly tired of leaving for work every morning at 7am with him tucked in bed and finding him in the same position when I returned. We would make up after fights, but soon repeat the same cycle. I suggested that we see a Christian counselor. He quickly told me that he did not believe in God, Christ, or anything else, and told me that *I* could pray about us.

I feel so alone, and am too ashamed to tell my family or friends about our situation. They all think that Robert works from home and that we are the perfect couple. How did I get myself into this mess? Disbelief, anger, sadness, embarrassment, and regrets haunt me, and every day I find myself *crying over spilt milk.*

Continuing the Conversation

We all have regrets. Because of our sin nature, individuals (even believers) make poor choices and choose to be led by the flesh and not by the spirit of God. Regrets can leave you feeling discouraged, shamed, saddened, disillusioned, and just plain stupid. Like any other difficult situation, we have a choice: to embrace, learn, and grow or despise, deny, and repeat the mistake.

1. Be alert and take responsibility. Often when we are living through a regretful situation, we feel that the circumstance was forced on us, but much like amusement park attractions, we chose to take the ride; no one forced us. In fact, most of the time there was a large sign before we entered the ride clearly stating the hazards. If we are honest, usually family and friends have warned us, but we did not take heed. Disregarding the warnings, we made a decision to enter into that relationship, to take that job, or to say and do as we pleased. Taking ownership of our poor choices, mistakes, and sins is the first step toward healing. (Matthew 26:41, Proverbs 3:5-6)

2. Sometimes we have to wait until the lesson has been learned. Friends told us the ride was scary, we read the hazard sign at the entrance, and stood in line for hours to finally get on the ride. We were having a great time until we hit the first 360-degree loop. We screamed, clutched the person next to us, cried out, and wished we could get off the ride. Well, most rides will not stop to let you off until it is over. And, most circumstances don't automatically cease because we are hurt and ready to get out of them. On the amusement park ride, we have to hold on to the rail until the ride stops. In real life, we have to

hold on to the Word of God, Christian family and friends until our trial is over or learn to live with our situation. (Romans 5:3-5)

3. Try to learn from the mistake and/or sin that caused the regret. Seek the Bible for counsel on life issues and follow it. The Bible is relevant even in the 21st century and is apropos for every situation. Christian counseling can also be a powerful tool to help you personally navigate during challenging times. (II Timothy 2:15, Proverbs 24:6b)

4. *Don't Cry Over Spilt Milk.* You made the mistake; accept it, and move forward. God's mercies are new every morning (Lamentations 3:22-23). God can take a bad situation and turn it into something good for those who love and are committed to Him (Romans 8:28). Remember, you are not the first or the last person to make a mistake. Unfortunately, it's part of being human. Confess to God, for He is quick to forgive (I John 1:9). And don't forget to forgive yourself.

Let's Think About It

What are you still crying over? What are you going to do about it?

_____

_____

_____

_____

_____

_____

_____

_____

_____

_____

_____

_____

_____

_____

_____

_____

_____

I Want More

I was really happy for her. She had been my best friend for years and we really had done life together. We had shared twenty years of birthdays, anniversaries, pedicures, tears, and laughter. So when she and her husband finally purchased their dream home, I wondered why I felt so gloomy. Again, I was happy for her, but I was deeply saddened. Was it because after 20 years of marriage, we were still living in a two bedroom cookie cutter house with the same cardboard furniture that I had in college? My best friend and her husband had his and her Lexuses, of course, while my husband and I had his and her clunkers that I was embarrassed to be seen in. Why do *we* have to struggle so hard?

My husband and I chose professions that we enjoyed. Was that foolish? We are very fulfilled in our careers, but there is no fulfillment in our bank accounts. We are both educators, a high school history teacher and a middle school football coach at public schools, but did we take into consideration that teachers only made so much? Our decision that I would stay at home with the kids when they were young didn't help our finances either. I was thankful for the time with our children, however, now when I look at what my friends have, I constantly wonder if we made the right decision.

When we were invited to my friend's housewarming party, I conveniently came down with the stomach flu. What would my housewarming gift look like, anyway? I'm sure my Walmart crock pot would be a great addition in their custom home. More and more I am feeling dissatisfied with life. Why? We have a house, food, and clothes. Nonetheless, I want more. Is this all God has for me? Why do others appear to prosper while John and I work hard but have so very little to show for our efforts? Does God love us, too?

Continuing the Conversation

Unfortunately, we live in a world where Wall Street, celebrities, reality TV, and social media have promoted the feeling that if we don't have the right car, house, or clothes, then we're nothing. We constantly compare our lives to Facebook postings that are often a snapshot and not the full-length movie of a person's life. If Wall Street, cable TV, Twitter, or our friends are the standards, we will always fall short. Someone will always have more or better "stuff." Contentment is a choice.

1. God does not promise that everyone is going to be rich, even His saints. He promises food and clothing. There is nothing wrong with having resources, but the world can make a person feel that true happiness can only come from constantly pursuing "things," which is a lie from Satan. (I Timothy 6:7-8)

2. Discontentment can lead to sin. The Bible says "some people eager for money have wandered from the faith and pierced themselves with many griefs." Many Christians have found themselves suffering the consequences of trying to keep up with the Joneses. (I Timothy 6:10)

3. Things will not make you happy; only a growing relationship with God through Christ Jesus will bring true joy. (I Timothy 6:6)

4. Don't worry; God knows exactly what you need and finds pleasure in sometimes providing some of our wants and desires. (Matthew 6:25-26)

5. Enjoy your life. Be thankful for what really matters. God wants us to live a life of gratitude for what He has given us. (I Thessalonians 5:18)

6. Be content with God's plan for your life. Paul states that he has learned to be content in every situation. (Philippians 4: 11-13)

Let's Think About It

What things are you depending on to make you happy? Are these "things" bringing consistent peace and joy into your life?

_____

_____

_____

_____

_____

_____

_____

_____

_____

_____

_____

_____

_____

_____

_____

RUNNING ON EMPTY

*O*ften life is such a whirlwind, I forget to stop and put gas in my vehicle. When my husband gets into my car, he is often exasperated because he wonders why I chose to "run on empty." I tell him that other people, things, and activities were priorities. They needed me. He regularly lets me know that if I don't take the time to ensure I have enough gasoline in my car, it will eventually hinder how I can care for anyone else (because I will be on the side of the road needing assistance, myself). I'm embarrassed to admit that this has happened to me a couple of times.

Often we run our lives in the same way. Instead of first filling our spiritual gas tank by spending time with Christ, Bible study, and prayer, we spend precious time ripping and running around, doing all the stuff for others that we think is important, while neglecting the most important part of our existence. We hold the expectation that people and activities will bring fullness, and when they don't, we feel even emptier.

When running on empty, we may try to get our husbands to fill the void by expecting them to be the perfect mate. We are inevitably disappointed when he does not take out the trash, or forgets to pay a bill, leaves his clothes all over the bedroom floor, or does not intently listen to the recap of the saga of your best friend (for the third time).

When running on empty, we might look for fulfillment in our children, expecting our kids to be flawless. But we are bound to be disappointed when they are disobedient, disrespectful, or ungrateful in their immaturity. It's easy to think, "After all that I have done for these kids, they are not appreciative. My tank is still empty."

We depend on our friends for a gallon or two of gas to fill our emotional tank. After all, we have kept their kids, brought them food, and cleaned their homes when they were sick. We've even chauffeured them to doctors' appointments and listened to countless late night troubles. We are certain our friends will understand and offer much needed relief, until you discover that they have forgotten your birthday, didn't call when you were ill, and overlooked the RSVP for your fabulous fiftieth birthday party.

When all else fails, a shopping spree or a new activity always pleases. A designer handbag with matching designer shoes and scarf should do it. A membership to one of the best country clubs in town affords a plethora of activities. Everything is wonderful until the credit card bill arrives, leaving us running on empty *and* in debt.

Continuing the Conversation

Husbands, children, and friends will never be able to completely fulfill us. How do I trust God to keep my tank filled? Adhere to the following recommendations, and soon your tank will soon be topped off!

1. Pursue disciplines of a Godly life. Accept Christ as your personal Savior and Lord, pray, study your Bible, fellowship with the saints, daily commit your walk to Christ. (Romans 12:1-2)

2. Seek a life that is pleasing to God. Allow the Bible and Holy Spirit to be your guide. (I Thessalonians 4:1)

3. Make daily decisions to put Christ first and seek Him (not people or things) when you are feeling empty. (Matthew 6:33)

4. Trust that God knows exactly what you need to feel complete. (Romans 15:13)

5. Give expecting nothing in return. Don't place demands on people to make you happy. Only a growing relationship with God through Jesus Christ can bring ultimate fulfillment and joy. (Psalm 16:11)

Let's Think About It

What are you filling your tank with on a daily basis? Is it bringing you total fulfillment?

_____

_____

_____

_____

_____

_____

_____

_____

_____

_____

_____

_____

_____

_____

_____

_____

HAS GOD FORGOTTEN ME?

The first wedding was fun. I couldn't wait to celebrate with one of my besties. I was so happy for my friend and the great guy God had sent her. The second wedding was nice, too. I went to New York for the bachelorette party and danced all night celebrating my friend's new union. By the third nuptial, I noticed that there were 25 single ladies trying to catch the bride's bouquet, but only three guys out on the floor when the groom threw the garter, and one of them was 12 years old! But it was still ok, because my best friend and I were still single, and though we had dreams of marrying that perfect guy, we were still enjoying our singlehood. That all changed when my best friend, Jill, met Paul. And all of a sudden, I was enjoying the single life alone. Single but not satisfied; happy for her but not so much for me. At their wedding, I went through all the right motions, said all the right things, but all the while I was thinking, "Has God forgotten me?"

Eventually, I bounced back and knew God had a

special man for me. After all, I was smart, attractive, had a successful career, and loved the Lord. All I needed to do was to get out to meet more people. I purposefully joined two singles groups and one small group, started working out at a popular gym (only cute workout clothes), and made a point to always look attractive. I even lost 10 pounds.

Through the years, I dated several guys, but none were the right fit. I have tried to be content as a single woman. I enjoy the freedom in my life and take every opportunity to be spontaneous and maximize this season. I intellectually know that I am complete in Christ and that God is enough to fill my heart, but to be honest, sometimes it doesn't feel like it. I keep trying to fill my longing with plans, friends, and activities, but often I still feel unfulfilled. What am I doing wrong?

It's hard to believe 10 years have passed. My friends in weddings 1, 2, 3, and 4 all have children, houses, and family vacations. If one more person (including my parents) asks me when I am going to get married, I'm going to scream. I'm 44, still unmarried, and thinking, "Has God forgotten me?"

Continuing the Conversation

It can be very discouraging when everyone around you appears to have something that you desire. Sometimes it's hard to believe that God has a perfect plan for our lives when He does not grant our wants and desires. Be encouraged; God never forgets his children.

1. God has a perfect plan for you. The plan for your life is perfect because God is perfect, in total control, and loves us more than we could ever imagine. (Jeremiah 29:11, Psalm 139:16)

2. Pray, fast, and ask God to send you a godly mate. Fasting and prayer is a spiritual tool that Christians can use to draw closer to God. Usually, fasting is defined by going without food or drink for a specified period of time. But a believer can fast from anything that the flesh (body) desires, craves, or enjoys; such as, television, music, Facebook, etc. Jesus declared in Matthew 17:21 that sometimes we will only experience a break-through by praying and fasting.

3. Cultivate a spirit of thanksgiving. Continue to thank and praise God even when He says, "no" or, "wait," trusting that he has something better in store for you. (I Thessalonians 5:18)

4. Make the most of this season in your life by serving God and growing spiritually. Singlehood can be a joyous time of life, knowing that you can fully focus on others, ministry,

THOMAS, RANDLE AND SMITH

and yourself without the distractions of spouses and children. (Ephesians 2:10)

5. Trust that God is working in your life. (Psalm 9:10, Psalm 56:3)

Let's Think About It

What are some of your wants and desires? Are you willing to trust God's will and timing in your life?

_____

_____

_____

_____

_____

_____

_____

_____

_____

_____

_____

_____

_____

_____

_____

SOMETIMES I THINK I'M UNIQUE, BUT THEN I REMEMBER I'M NOT . . .

It was 40 years ago, the first loss. My brother Steve died. He was 22 and I was 18. How could I handle this terrible loss? Not so much for me as for my mom. After his death, I remember thinking that I would write. I would put all my thoughts and feelings on paper. I thought I would write how I felt about Steve and what happened, but it was difficult to bring it together. With not much time to grieve, me, my mom and younger siblings were on our way to celebrate my high school graduation with a cross-country drive. Little did I know, this trip would be a part of the grieving process. We went to Greenville, South Carolina where Steve's family lived. We didn't have the same father. We were going to meet his father's family. Steve never met this man, but he did know his name and that he was stationed at Fulton Airforce base. My mom was a senior in high school when she became pregnant with Steve. This fact was interesting, but yielded no answers to my many questions.

Why was I getting to meet my brother's dad's family, who he never met? After 22 years, they welcomed us into their home. It seemed strange to me, but for some reason my mom wanted us to connect with them. All those years, I had rationalized that my brother's family was probably poor, uneducated, and could not really help my mom or brother financially or otherwise and that was why Steve never heard from them. To my chagrin, that was far from reality. Steve's paternal family was very well off, upper middle class, and well respected in the community. Why had they not shared their life with Steve? Why did they act as though Steve did not exist? Sometimes death brings more questions than answers.

The second loss was my youngest sister. I'll never forget the day of her diagnosis. I went from being the big sister who gave way too much sisterly advice, to playing the role of a parent to her kids. It was an exhausting adventure. My new normal included cooking meals, picking up children from school, and going to parent-teacher conferences, including the alternative school for my nephew. I wasn't comfortable with my nephew's educational situation, and didn't want to be.

I have been known for taking lots of pictures, but I have none of that time. Maybe I didn't want to remember it. This was my mom's youngest child, her youngest daughter. My mom protected her like a momma bear would guard her cub. I took a year to grieve after her death. I remember not talking about her death much, but pouring myself into any project I embarked upon. As soon as I felt I was in a good place, I moved on. And then the unthinkable happened again.

The third loss was my youngest brother, Chad. Yes, my mom had six children, and three of them have passed away. Chad and I had a special relationship. He had taken on the role of protector for my mom. We shared a lifetime of memories in the few short years between his cancer diagnosis and his death. I remember feeling so helpless, but never hopeless, when Chad got sick. Our hugs became so special and his "I love you" made me feel a true sense of a brother's love. He made me laugh until the end. He would always play jokes on us, and you couldn't get mad at him because you fell for it over and over again. I love telling his story.

Chad loved life and he even admitted he didn't want to die. I can vividly remember crying out to the Lord to please spare his life, to leave him here. How could God allow my mom to lose another child? Chad helped me make peace with that. I remember a conversation in which he boldly proclaimed, "On this side or the other, I'm in a good place! I'm ready for whatever the Lord has for me."

Seven years before his death, Chad had rededicated his life to the Lord and would tell everyone who would listen how good his God was. In his last days, I saw such maturity in a man who took the time to bring each of us close and share a word of encouragement, edification, or rebuke when needed.

When I think of Chad, I have to laugh, because that's what he made us do. I may not be able to replace my lost siblings, but I can enjoy the memories and my remaining family members.

Continuing the Conversation

The pain of loss and the strain of family problems can threaten to steal our joy and motivation in life, but if you turn to God, He can bring something beautiful from the hardship.

1. His ways are not our ways. In life, often we do not understand why God allows painful losses. Don't waste precious time on asking why, but instead focus on your Christian walk and pleasing God. (Isaiah 55:8)

2. There can be growth in pain. We have all heard the term "growing pains" in reference to both physical and organizational growth. Christians can also have growing pains during times of spiritual growth. Remember that emotional pain is temporary, and true healing can only come through our relationship with Christ. (II Corinthians 4:16)

3. All families have a few "issues." Focus on the positive attributes in your family unit and not on the issues. Try to be the model for encouragement and family unity (even when others are not cooperating). Develop and maintain a spirit of thanksgiving for your family, accepting them for who they are. (Ephesians 5:20)

Let's Think About It

How would you characterize your relationship with your siblings/family? Are you pursuing long-lasting, positive relationships with family members?

_____

_____

_____

_____

_____

_____

_____

_____

_____

_____

_____

_____

_____

_____

_____

SPICY

Colorful and Zesty Conversations

THE WOUND OF WORDS

The wound of words is worse than the wound of swords.
~ Saudi Arabian Proverb

I always knew he was not my real dad. I'm not sure how, but I knew. Had I overheard an adult conversation? Had I accidentally read a confidential letter? I don't remember, but I knew that I should never repeat the fact. I didn't quite look like him, but neither did I look like my mom. He always treated me like a beloved daughter, and I called him "Dad." After all, he was the only father I had ever known. I rarely thought about who my real dad was or where he was. For all practical and emotional purposes this "dad" was my real dad and we had a wonderful relationship. He took me to swim practice, played dolls with me, and taught me how to drive. I even thought that one day I would marry someone just like him.

He really loved my mom. They regularly showed

public affection to one another, and mother loved being called Mrs. Franko. My last name was also Franko. Everyone in our little town assumed Mr. Franko was my dad. Did he adopt me? I'm not quite sure and I never asked. But I was grateful for his love and support in our lives, and couldn't imagine life without him. I never once wished that he wasn't my "dad" or resented his position as my parent. Which is why I am shocked that as an adult I reacted to a simple spat with such a harsh response.

I was 22 and home from college one sunny afternoon in June. There was a simple request from my dad, a disrespectful remark from me, a stern reprimand from my dad, then I announced publicly in front of all our family and friends, "Who do you think you are? You're not my real dad!" I can still see my dad's hurt face and the shock of all those around us, especially my mom. Did I really say that? How I wish I could take those words back. What would make me explode with such a hurtful statement toward someone I love?

Continuing the Conversation

All of us have said things we wish we could take back. The tongue is one of the most difficult members of our body to control. Let's look at a few ways to tame this sometimes wild beast. (James 3:8)

1. Don't hold a conversation when you are angry. Often, when we are angry, we are not thinking rationally. Most people say hurtful things when they are angry. The Bible says, "be slow to speak and quick to hear." (James 1:19) When we are upset, we are usually quick to speak and slow to hear because we are trying to get our point across and/or hurt our opponent. Resume the conversation once everyone has calmed down with the mindset to resolve the issue. (Proverbs 21:23)

2. Remember that our opponent is not flesh and blood. (Ephesians 6:12) When you find yourself upset and tempted to retaliate verbally, take a deep breath and understand that Satan could very well be using you, that person, situation, or misunderstanding to cause disunity in the body of Christ.

3. Words do hurt and can leave long-standing wounds. Once you say something hurtful to an individual, you can and should ask for forgiveness, but you cannot retrieve the words. Words hurt just as much, if not more than, physical wounds. Think about this the next time you decide to give someone "a piece of your mind." (James 1:26, Proverbs 18:21)

Let's Think About It

Who have you wounded with your words? What are you going to do about it?

_____

_____

_____

_____

_____

_____

_____

_____

_____

_____

_____

_____

_____

_____

TOO TIRED, AKA I NEED A WIFE, TOO

I pull in our driveway, but I'm too tried to get out the car. I finally muster up enough energy to step out of the car and walk through the door. I would love to collapse on the sofa with a cup of tea and just relax. Then my reality sets in; the kids are hungry, the laundry is overflowing, the dog (they wanted) needs to be walked. Not to mention homework, school lunch prep, dirty dishes, and the cake that my husband needs for his office potluck tomorrow. I put on my mommy hat, wife scarf, and begin.

Little did I know, I would soon have to add my employee belt, my neighbor boots, and my relative gloves. The phone rings and it is my sister who is newly divorced and needs me to babysit this weekend because she needs to work an extra shift to bring in additional income. My boss texts to ask if I could send him the latest financial reports (for the third time), and the neighbor down the street needs the proverbial cup of sugar. I just want to stop and have an emotional breakdown but I don't have time.

Around 10pm the last dish is dried, the kids are in

bed, and I'm so ready to retire. As I am showering and getting ready for bed, my husband gives me that look. I know what that look means. So, I am not off yet; my shift has not ended. I find myself rummaging through my lingerie drawer to find a teddy that still fits.

Don't get me wrong, I love my kids and husband. I will gladly get every task accomplished, but has anyone even slightly considered me? I feel that all the people I love want more and more from me. Is anyone interested in what I need? If I am everyone's help, who is my help?

Continuing the Conversation

Living in a fallen world can be very demanding. Have you ever felt overwhelmed, wondering if anyone really cares about you? Remember that you are not alone. There is an ever-present source of comfort.

1. God does care deeply for us. When feeling overwhelmed, remember that God is the perfect comforter. (Isaiah 46:4, I Peter 5:7)

2. Schedule regular respite time. Intentionally schedule time for rest and relaxation. You will not be able to effectively minister to your family if you are exhausted mentally and physically. (Mark 6:31)

3. Learn to say no. Ask God for wisdom before agreeing to help extended family or friends. Consider reevaluating your career if it constantly causes stress and exhaustion or leaves little time for family. (James 1:5)

Let's Think About It

Am I consistently stretching myself too thin? Do I plan time for rest and relaxation in my schedule?

_____

_____

_____

_____

_____

_____

_____

_____

_____

_____

_____

_____

_____

_____

_____

_____

_____

MAN IN THE MIDDLE

$\mathcal{I}$ enjoy window shopping with my grown daughter, Lynn. We love to wander through shopping malls talking, laughing, and looking. On one of these occasions, between trying on sweaters and sunglasses, a woman approached me and asked if my name was Carol and if this was my daughter, and then proceeded to ask my daughter's age. I felt like her questions were a little strange but she looked harmless. She then shared that she had a daughter the same age as mine and asked if she could share her story, which eventually became our story.

We found a spot in the mall's food court and she began. "I was young, sweet, and innocent and he was handsome, charming, and about 10 years my senior. You know, all the things that great love stories are made of. He loved me and I loved him. So when I became pregnant, I was not worried because I knew we would be married, raise our child and live happily ever after.

Unfortunately, for me, that did not happen. Soon I

began to wonder why he didn't want to marry quickly before I started showing. As I entered my seventh month, I concluded that he wanted to wait until after the baby was born to have a proper wedding. More and more, we could not be together as much as I wanted because he was always working. As with most babies, I went into labor during the night and for some strange reason, he could not take me to the hospital. Thank God for my mom and best girlfriend. My love finally arrived at the hospital the next morning two hours before our beautiful baby girl, Bria, was born. I knew everything was going to be all right.

As soon as I recovered from childbirth, I started planning our wedding again. One evening as I was sharing the details of my upcoming nuptials with my sister, I discovered she had details of her own to share with me, and they were even more painful than my recent delivery. She heard that my guy was married and had another daughter a little older than Bria. I really did not believe her at first. I trusted this guy, loved this guy, and he had promised to marry me. But after the initial shock, I did a little more investigating and found out that all of it was true. I had ignored all the tale-tale signs, but now everything made sense. The infrequency of his visits, not being able to hang out in public places, his inability to follow through on his marriage promise, and even his much delayed arrival to the hospital for the birth of our child.

My emotions ranged from denial and disillusionment to hurt and anger. They finally settled on revenge. I wanted my guy to feel all the hurt, embarrassment, and shame that I was feeling. It was simple, I would arrive unannounced at a neighborhood dance club that he owned, where locals frequented to dance, socialize, and have a few drinks. I took my uncle's pistol with the intent to only confront and embarrass him in front of everyone. I walked in and took a table in the back and waited until he noticed me. When our eyes met, I started to pull out the pistol and then I saw this beautiful toddler run across the room. I stood up and immediately placed it back in my purse and ran out the door. Being a mother myself, I was terrified at the thought of accidently hurting an innocent child or her parents in an attempt to "get even."

After a brief silence, she stopped telling her story and stared at Lynn and me with tears in her eyes. Looking at my daughter, she then shared that Lynn was the little girl who ran across the room that night. We instantly understood that Lynn and Bria were both the daughters of my ex-husband. After another silence that seemed like an eternity, we embraced. Two women deceived by the same man.

Continuing the Conversation

An age old story, boy meets girl, boy and girl fall in love, girl gets pregnant, girl wants to marry, boy is already married, and girl wants revenge. Too often in our fallen world, this is reality. What can we do to avoid deceitful people and unhealthy relationships? What do we do when we find ourselves dealing with the consequences of sinful behavior?

1. Daily ask God for discernment in all of life's issues. Discernment is the ability to judge well. Often we can become blinded to sin because of our desires. (Romans 12:2, Philippians 1:9-10)

2. In our flesh, we automatically want to hurt those who have hurt us. In His Word, God states, "vengeance is mine; I will repay." I know it does not sound very comforting, but forgive and trust God to fight your battles. He doesn't need your help. (Deuteronomy 32:35, Romans 12:19)

3. In our earthly eyes, our situation can look bleak and hopeless. But we know a God that specializes in turning our worst circumstances into blessings. He can even make up for time, emotions, and resources lost. (Joel 2:25, Romans 8:28)

Let's Think About It

Is there a situation or a person in your past or present that left you feeling like you need to seek revenge? What is the Biblical response?

_____

_____

_____

_____

_____

_____

_____

_____

_____

_____

_____

_____

_____

_____

_____

DISILLUSIONED

I have such fond memories of New Hope Missionary Baptist Free Church, where my grandfather was one of the founding members. I can remember, as though it was yesterday, his long, drawn-out prayers and him leading spirit-filled hymns at the church altar. My father was a deacon and my mother was head of the mothers' board. It was understood that I would be an active member when I returned from college, and I did not disappoint.

I returned from college with a BS and a MRS and my husband and I formally took the right-hand of fellowship (joined the church) and began serving in a ministry. My husband and I were faithful tithers and felt honored to support a ministry with such sentimental ties. Annually, the church held a business meeting to allow the congregation to review and have input into the church's budget. My husband, an accountant by trade, always looked forward to these meetings because it gave him an opportunity to use his gifts and ensure that the church was maintaining best practices in the area of financial integrity. With his CPA intellect, he always had a good report of the church's finances.

Last year, we noticed that the annual business meeting had been postponed. The church leadership told us that it would be rescheduled soon, but a year passed with no business meeting. We were sure this was just an oversight. Life happens, even with spiritual people. As time went on, we noticed that no announcements were made and no further business meetings were scheduled. My husband, the consummate professional accountant, began feeling uneasy and started to question the lack of financial transparency. In a meeting with the church business manager he discovered that the leadership was no longer comfortable with sharing the church's financial information.

This really troubled both of us, but especially my husband. He quickly scheduled a meeting with the Deacon Board, but to his dismay, the deacons politely told him that they ran the church and for him to mind his own business. Feeling that this was Biblically wrong, we decided to take our concern to our parents and other long-time members to glean some support. When the leadership discovered that we had discussed the situation with others in the congregation, we received a certified letter asking us to leave the church.

We read this letter at least 20 times, not believing that

it could be true. My grandfather started that church. My friends and family were at that church. We had served with our time and resources. How could we be asked to leave?

Continuing the Conversation

Sometimes life situations, even in the church, can catch you off guard. Expectations can be destroyed or deflated, and people are not always who you want them to be. Situations can leave us deeply wounded or scarred. Let's discuss how we can begin healing our wounds.

1. There is no perfect church, place, or situation. Because of the original man's fall (Adam), we were all born with a sinful nature. Understanding this truth will help you to cope and eventually forgive. (Romans 5:12)

2. Unfortunately, in this life, people will disappoint and hurt you, both intentionally and unintentionally. Many individuals have been hurt because they expected people to always be kind, honest, and fair. Jesus is the only person who never disappoints. (Hebrews 13:5-6)

3. The Bible instructs us to pray for those who mistreat us and that vengeance is the Lord's. Follow the principle in Matthew 18:15-17 by trying first to resolve the conflict by initially discussing it with the individuals involved, realizing that you may not get the response expected.

(Hebrews 10:30)

4. When bad things happen, we have a choice to forgive, heal, and move forward, or to sulk and hold grudges. The later only hinders and destroys you and does not leave room for you to experience the fullness of life that God has in store for you. (Matthew 6:14-15)

Let's Think About It

Have your expectations been shattered by another person/organization/ministry? How will you move on?

_____

_____

_____

_____

_____

_____

_____

_____

_____

_____

_____

_____

_____

_____

_____

CHANGE AGENT

$\mathcal{F}$inally, I had my turn walking down the aisle. My husband-to-be loved the Lord, was handsome, and had a great job. Did I mention he was eye candy? We honeymooned in Mexico and spent the first few months enjoying being Mr. and Mrs. Williams. But it's amazing how living under the same roof suddenly revealed some of Mr. William's inadequacies that I had not noticed before. But I was not discouraged; I knew I could help him improve. I felt that our marriage would be even better if I could only change a few things in him.

Thing number one. He had a great job as an engineer, but I thought he could make more money and have more flexibility if he had his own business. I refused to accept that he did not have or desire to have an entrepreneurial spirit. He enjoyed working hard and letting the buck stop somewhere else. But knowing what was best for my man, I convinced him to resign and pursue opening his own engineering firm.

Thing number two. Mr. Williams loved serving in the

children' s ministry at church and working with the youth, but my friend's husband who teaches the adults had just been asked to be in leadership training. I thought my husband needed to be a leader in the church and I could help him. He shared with me that he had no desire to be in leadership now, but wanted to continue growing himself and working with the youth. I was not listening to what he thought.

Thing number three. I constantly wondered when he was going to grow up. He spent every other weekend hanging out with his old college buddies, or should I say, his boys. Those guys were fine, but I wanted him to spend more time polishing himself. Instead of basketball, why not golf? Instead of spades and dominoes, why not chess?

Thing number four. Did I share that I have a MBA? I know what's best for our home, our finances, and our future. So I let Mr. Williams know that he did not have to worry about those things and that I would handle all decisions and let him know what was decided.

I was shocked when he told me, after two years of marriage, that he was very unhappy with his business, church leadership, learning how to play chess, and most of all, me. He wondered why I never encouraged his dreams or if his desires even mattered.

Continuing the Conversation

Too late, I remembered that these were all my passions, and not my husbands. I thought I was encouraging him to be better, but I was really just pushing him to be different. I never thought to ask him how God was leading him or what he wanted. Why was I trying to change him?

1. We are not our husband's Holy Spirit. We cannot force our preferences on others, even our mates. Pray, encourage, set a good example, and allow God's spirit to do the work. (I Peter 3:1)

2. We all have been given different gifts. Celebrate the gifts that God has already placed in your spouse. Every gift is important in the body of Christ. (Romans 12: 6-8, I Corinthians 12:14)

3. Women were created by God to be their husband's helpmate. God gave us our mates so we could complete one another, not remake one another. (I Corinthians 11:3, Genesis 2:18)

4. It is commanded in the Bible that wives respect their husbands. This commandment can be very difficult in a world where "narcissism" is the norm. Look for ways to

show respect on a daily basis. For instance, regularly prepare your husband's favorite meal, complete his requests, and compliment him privately and publicly. (Ephesians 5:33)

Let's Think About It

Is there an individual in your life that you are trying to make-over? How do you know what is best for them?

_____

_____

_____

_____

_____

_____

_____

_____

_____

_____

_____

_____

_____

_____

SWEET

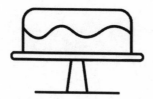

Pleasant and Satisfying Conversations

Our Gifting

$\mathcal{I}$ marvel at the gifts God so graciously bestows. We are each born with Divine giftings that are not only meant to be shared with those around us, but also instilled in our children. Our childhood experiences play a big role in the person we become. The next passage shares how gifts can be passed on to future generations.

A Recipe for a Good Life

Food is a part of the earliest memory I have of my mom.

Holidays were filled with love, warmth, family, and lots of food. I can't remember a time when my mom wasn't entertaining, hosting a dinner, or giving an impromptu party. As a result, I have incorporated those things into my life; it's part of my imprinting. It's amazing how we grow to love the things that we grow up with. My mother, affectionately known as "Granny" since the birth of her first grandchild in 1976, has made an impact on each of her children's lives.

There were always cloth napkins set on our table and

the table was set for each family meal. My mom treated each of us like we were guests. A salad plate was usually a part of our table setting, though not always welcomed by the children (for many reasons—dish duty not being the least of them). My mom could mess up all the dishes in the kitchen making one meal. To this day I call my mom to get advice for setting the table properly, even though I could Google it. It amazes me how she can rattle place settings off like she wrote the book, even though she is self-taught.

She makes a simple dinner seem like a feast for the elite. What she does at the dinner table speaks volumes to me, my siblings, and all who experience it. My sister and I leave her table marveling at how her chicken tastes, like it has been marinated in special spices to tempt the palate for a lingering drift into foodie heaven. It's simply love, salt and pepper. My mom makes a pound cake that will make you want to retire your recipe; it's the best. Sometimes I consider entering her mouthwatering creations into a contest, but the selfish part of me doesn't want to share!

We grew up in a very modest setting. There was plenty, in my eyes, but now I know that Granny made the most of a hard situation. I remember Sundays when the youth from our church, all of them it seems, would come to our house and she would make a meal out of whatever was in her cabinets. It was her ministry then, and still is at 80 years old. She still cooks and delivers food to her friends and the shut in.

My mom seemed to always be there, but she wasn't. She had to work to support her six children. At an early age, I remember my brothers walking her down the railroad tracks to her job. She worked in the food industry. Later, she worked in private homes as a cook. Today we might call her a Private Chef, but then she was simply "The Help."

I grew up at the feet of an amazing chef. I suffer from nearness to greatness. I often eat other people's food and think, "Granny should teach them how to cook." Smells of baked goods, roasted meats, and hearty vegetables color my memory. You name it, she made it. Her talent is generational; it is her legacy. Her grandchildren cook and most have learned at her stove.

It's interesting to watch her as she still mentors from afar. Family gatherings now don't consist of all of her dishes anymore, but I know many calls go out the night before with questions of "Granny how much of this or that?" and "How long and what temperature?"

My mom is short in stature and has a petite frame, but what a wealth of knowledge and experience she holds within. She can set a table for a King. God has given her an incredible ability, her gift of hospitality. Through food she has touched so many, and I will always love and treasure the time I have spent sitting at her feet. She has a small bend in her back and her hands bear the scars of arthritis, but it takes a lot to keep her from preheating her oven or turning on the gas top to prepare a meal for her family or someone in need.

She always called us her gang or her monsters, but we knew there was nothing she wouldn't do for us. Every time this monster heads to my kitchen and turns on my stove to feed my family, I know that I honor her and the gift of hospitality that she instilled in me. She is Granny, she is mom, she is mine, and I love her.

Continuing the Conversation

What legacy do you want to leave your family? What legacy are you intentionally passing on to your children? Creating and maintaining a home that honors God and others takes work. How do we show our children that serving and ministering to others is close to God's heart?

1. Intentionally leave a godly legacy. Let your children see you reading the Bible, praying, and making godly decisions on television programming and music enjoyment. Teach your children Biblical truths on various matters to instill godly character traits. (Psalm 78:4, Deuteronomy 6: 5-7)

2. Set goals and become very deliberate about what you are trying to instill in your children. Have regular devotional time and pray with your children. Worship at a Bible teaching church that emphasizes spiritual growth. In

addition, instill specific skills in your children that are important to you; such as, baking, gardening, etc. (Proverbs 22:6)

3. Teach your children how to show hospitality to others. Regularly model how to serve others in front of your children. For example, invite others to your home to share meals, especially those who cannot do anything for you in return. Have your family visit a local ministry or homeless shelter to deliver toys and food. (Hebrews 13:2, I Peter 4:9)

Let's Think About It

What are your gifts and how are you sharing them with your children and others to leave a godly legacy for future generations?

_____

_____

_____

_____

_____

_____

_____

_____

_____

_____

_____

_____

_____

_____

_____

TIME WILL NOT ERASE

I think about her almost every day. While cooking, I remember how we each took $20, drove to Wal-Mart, purchased food, and cooked family dinners for a week. While working, I remember how she dropped everything to come and help me finish typing my school's self-study for our upcoming accreditation visit. While driving, I remember the many trips and family vacations we took together. We talked on the phone almost every day. We shopped together, had pedicures together, celebrated almost every family occasion together. We were even pregnant together; she had 3 boys and I had 3 girls, all the same ages. For 23 years, Janet and I were prayer partners, running buddies, confidants, and best friends.

But most of all, I remember how she encouraged me, how she loved me, and how she enjoyed life with me. I miss having someone always there to call at any hour to share the highs and lows of life. I knew she would always be in my corner telling me I could do it, I would make it; it would be ok, let me pray with you. On occasion, I would also get a gentle reprimand of, "Girl, that's not Christ-like," or, "Let's just see what the Word of God has to say about that."

After the Lord took her home, it was difficult to go to any social outing where girl friends would be together. I felt so alone, and somewhat jealous that others had friends and I did not have mine. After much prayer and time, God laid on my heart to celebrate the time we had together and that one of his special blessings to me was 23 years with a best friend.

Janet was always preparing for something. I remember we were having lunch in December of 1999, and she was telling me about her preparation for the year 2000. (Remember, the world was supposed to go crazy during Y2K). She had stored water, food, and clothes, and she was discussing how to purchase a generator. She stopped midway through the conversation and asked me what I was going to do to prepare. I just looked at her and said, "If this is our last month, week, or day, I want to just sit here and enjoy my friend." That ended the conversation on Y2K, and we had the best lunch ever!

Continuing the Conversation

Friendship is a special gift. I was blessed to share many years of my adult life with a very special friend who God suddenly called home. Let me share a few thoughts that helped me on my healing journey.

1. Allow yourself time to go through the grieving process. Losing someone you love is major. Though we know believers are with Christ, we still miss them, especially if they were a major part of our lives. Jesus knows how we are feeling. The Bible says Jesus wept when he found out that Lazarus had died. (John 11:25)

2. Be thankful and celebrate the time you had with your loved one. Having someone special in your life is a blessing from God, so appreciate and rejoice that God saw fit to bring that person into your life. (I Thessalonians 5:18, Colossians 3:15)

3. Focus on what God has planned for you. If you are still living, God still has a plan for you on earth. Ask God to show you the ministry he has in store for you. (Proverbs 16:9)

4. Enjoy your family and friends now! You never know when the Lord may decide to call your friend or family member home, so make an effort to spend time enjoying your loved ones on a regular basis. We live in a very hectic and fast-paced world. Make it a priority to schedule time in advance to spend with special people in your life. (John 10:10)

5. Cultivate new relationships. The Christian life is about a relationship with God and relationships with others. (Mark 12:30-31) Cultivate those relationships today. To have a friend, be a friend. (Proverbs 18:24)

Let's Think About It

Are you cultivating lasting relationships/friendships? Am I a good friend to others?

_____

_____

_____

_____

_____

_____

_____

_____

_____

_____

_____

_____

_____

_____

_____

_____

Never Too Late

I often dream of being a lawyer or an accountant. I was great at math in school and excelled on my high school debate team. But I didn't finish my college degree. My parents could not afford to pay for my college courses, so instead of getting loans, I decided to work. I soon married and poured myself into being a wife and raising a family. I feel as though I blew my chance and did not reach my full potential, and now, I think it is too late. I loved learning as a youth and still do to this day. God gave me a great mind, and I feel that I wasted it.

However, I did manage to slowly climb the virtual corporate ladder. At 50, I was finally promoted to a mid-management position that they were hiring 22-year-old college graduates for. I am good at my job and excel at work, but I cannot be proud of what I have accomplished, because I am always comparing it to the dream I never fulfilled. My current position feels like a pitiful substitution for the career that I envisioned for myself.

It doesn't help that most of the friends I grew up with

have college degrees. It's funny how it doesn't matter who is pursuing higher education when you are 18, but it seems to be a glaring difference 30 years later. Is it because they have larger houses in nicer neighborhoods, luxury cars, and annually take winter and summer vacations? No, I can honestly say no. It is not their social status or material possessions—the reason that I feel so inferior is because I feel like they achieved their goals, and I did not.

After some soul-searching and encouragement from friends and family, I started investigating various colleges that had programs for working adults. I soon became discouraged when I discovered that it would probably take me seven years to complete a bachelor's degree going to school part-time; I would almost be 58 years old when I finished. When sharing this with one of my friends, she looked me squarely in the face and said, "Well, in 7 years you will be 58 anyway (or with Jesus). Do you want to be 58 with a degree or without a degree?" At first, I thought my friend was being sort of flippant. But later that evening as I reflected on what my friend had said, I wanted to be 58 with the degree. Reaching for my goals and dreams does not have an expiration date. I am going to pursue my potential now, because it's never too late.

Continuing the Conversation

All of us have dreams that we want to fulfill. Unfortunately, real life situations can deter us from reaching our goals. Practically, how can we move forward, claiming all that God has for us?

1. It's never too late; God is faithful. If God still has you here, he is not finished with you. Pray that He will reveal to you the next step. (Lamentations 3:22-23)

2. The only way to eat an elephant is one bite at a time. Start on your journey. Stop procrastinating. Trust God to lead and guide you. (Psalm 32:8)

3. Get a prayer partner who will hold you accountable. (James 5:16b, I John 5:14)

4. Stay positive and don't get discouraged when it appears to take a long time to reach your goals. God's timing is not our timing. Learn to trust God and enjoy your journey. (Deuteronomy 4:29)

Let's Think About It

What do you think God wants you to accomplish during your lifetime? What steps have you made towards your goal?

_____

_____

_____

_____

_____

_____

_____

_____

_____

_____

_____

_____

_____

_____

Happy Anniversary

*B*abe,

Life is treating us well. I love this day more than any and I still vividly remember the day that it all began. Early that morning, it rained, it poured, and then it cleared up just in time for us to get to the church and not get wet. The setting was beautiful and we were ready. We had planned; the stage was set. It felt like that moment was everything I had dreamed of.

To this day, we don't have a wedding album, but it's ok because I have it etched in my mind; I don't think our special day could be captured and put in a book. Even though there are days I wish I could see the pictures, we really don't need them.

We were young and innocent in so many ways. We started this journey dreaming, and we still dream. We've also had a few nightmares along the way, but every day I wake up and thank God for you and each new day with you and I really mean that.

I was so proud to be changing my name that Saturday

evening. Family and friends from all over greeted us. We were orchestrating a major production. I know that there wasn't an empty seat, but to be honest, the faces of those who attended is a blur. I just remember entering the church and seeing you at the altar and I felt safe, as though God had opened heaven and sent me an angel. You were everything that I had wished for. I have never second-guessed the decision to marry you; you are the one for me. We have shared so many wonderful times and I love when we reflect on how our lives have been so full. Yes, we have had our share of heartaches, but they have only made us stronger. I could not have imagined what we, or our lives, would look 32 years later.

Here we are, two totally different people, but so very much the same. We still have so much to learn, so much to give, so much to share, and so much love that hasn't been explored. My prayer is that the time we have left is so much sweeter than any time we've had before, that we get to know each other in ways that we've never known, and that we will love like never before. I love you more today than yesterday, and I want to spend the rest of my life as your wife.

Love you sooooo much,

Me

Continuing the Conversation

God designed the blueprint for marriage. It can be heaven when couples follow the blueprint and hell when they don't. God gives us specific guidelines for a happy marriage. Let's look at a few.

1. Leave and cleave. No earthly person is more important than your spouse. Commit to your mate fully for life. (Genesis 2:24)

2. Husbands, love your wives. Christ loved the church unto death on the cross. Husbands should follow Christ's example and be willing to sacrifice for their wives. (Ephesians 5:25)

3. Wives, respect your husbands. Wives should honor and respect their husbands in every way. Be creative; think of tangible ways to honor your husband privately and publicly. Regularly fulfill his requests and become his biggest cheerleader. (Ephesians 5:22)

4. Grow spiritually, individually and as a couple. Schedule time for individual and couple prayer and Bible study. Worship and serve together at a local Bible teaching church of your choice. (II Peter 3:18)

Let's Think About It

How do you honor your mate? Are you committed to your mate for life?

_____

_____

_____

_____

_____

_____

_____

_____

_____

_____

_____

_____

_____

_____

LESSONS LEARNED

smile comes to my face when you ask me about being a mother. It's a joy. That's who I am, what I do, and what I love. My family is my priority. I have been blessed with a wonderful career, great friends, and many gifts and talents, but my first ministry is always my family.

On my parenting journey, I have several women who speak truth into my life; it's like a speedy oil change when I'm off kilter. I have also found that daily time with God is essential. When I'm spending quality time in the Word, I set the stage for how our home runs, when I'm off, they're off; when I'm on, they're on. Parenting is such a high calling, and it is my deepest desire to be a Christ-like model in front of my children. – Mother

As summer is coming to a close and the first day of school is just around the corner, I find myself reflecting. This is one of my favorite times of the year. I've been blessed to be able to minister to children for over twenty-seven years in various roles: as a principal, teacher, instructional specialist, and ministry leader. However, the single most important role I have held by far has been that of a parent. In each role, I have learned some valuable lessons throughout the years, but I believe that the most valuable lessons came through parenting my own three children. My girls are now adults, but I still remember those last days of summer when they were young and we were getting ready for yet another school year! Days were spent in a mad rush to shop for special school clothes and hunting feverishly for the perfect backpack. And don't forget the requisite reams of notebook paper, the pens and pencils that had to be just right, and the glue sticks and crayons! Those days are gone, but I now have the joy of watching my daughter and grandson prepare for the new school year. I help out as only a grandmother can do, and share some of what I've learned with her as she, like her mother before her, learns the ropes of parenting and school days.

Continuing the Conversation

Some of the lessons I learned as a parent came easy; others I learned the hard way. I'd like to take this time to reflect and share with you some of the most important lessons I've learned over the years.

1. I learned early in my parenting years that the Scriptures are the ultimate authority when it comes to parenting. Whenever I would wish I had a training guide for parents, God would always remind me that He had already supplied

guidance in His Word which Paul states is good for "teaching, training, reproof, for correction, for training in righteousness so that the man of God may be adequate, equipped for every good work" (II Timothy 3: 16 NIV). The Word of God contains Biblical principles that can be applied to each and every aspect of life, including raising godly children. Are you trying to teach your child the importance of choosing good friends? I Corinthians 15:33 says, "Do not be deceived; bad company corrupts good morals." Are you trying to instill a strong work ethic in your child? Proverbs 10:4 states, "Poor is he who works with a negligent hand, but the hand of the diligent makes rich."

2. Teach and expect obedience from your child. You will not be able to train your child emotionally, cognitively, or spiritually if he does not obey you or others placed in authority over him. As a parent, it is your responsibility to set clear, consistent, and developmentally appropriate rules for your child in your home as well as for your child when he is away from home. A vital aspect to remember is that learning is often *caught*, not *taught*. This means that children tend to follow what they *see* more than what they *hear*. Simply stating and enforcing the rules is not enough; as parents we have to model obedience to the Word of God and the authorities placed over us in front of our children. (Luke 6:40)

3. The goal of every parent is to raise responsible children. Far too often, well-meaning parents hinder their children from receiving natural consequences for inappropriate behavior. It's the teacher's fault the homework did not get turned in. It's the coach's fault that your child did not make the team. You want your child to be able to function successfully and become self-disciplined. Children can be given responsibilities as early as age three with simple tasks such as picking up toys, helping mommy clean off the table after dinner, and straightening up their rooms before bed. By the age of eight, your child should be able to set his own alarm clock, be able to get himself up, get dressed, and be ready for school on time. (Proverbs 22:6)

4. Enjoy your children. "Children are a gift from the Lord." (Psalm 127:3-4 NIV) I know there may be times your child doesn't feel like a gift – the colicky nights, the trips to the doctor, or the discipline we often have to meter out as our children grow and mature, all on top of the busy and exhausting pace of life. Often it may seem as if it takes all your energy to simply feed and bathe your child and then tuck him into bed after a long day. It can be a challenge to set aside time from your busy schedule to spend time with your children, yet I urge you to do it. Second only to God and your spouse, the relationship with your children is the most important relationship you will have on this Earth. You were intended to disciple and grow them into

responsible Kingdom citizens. Building relationships involves spending time together. Spend time each day just talking with your child. This is not time to lecture but to sincerely ask about their day and share some things about your day if appropriate. Plan ahead for family nights and *schedule* them. Put them on your calendar as you would any appointment. I remember Family Night at our house was every Friday night. We would play board games, watch movies, go bowling, or have devotion as a family. It was during those times we grew the most as a family unit.

5. Remember, your role as a parent is a serious call from God and His gift to you. You only have a short window of time to prepare your child to be a responsible Christian citizen who will make a difference in a secular world. It can be a daunting task, but God has provided everything we need as parents to raise godly children. Pray, study the Word of God, and build relationships with each other and with other Christian parents that will hold you accountable. You are training and discipling the future generation of Kingdom builders.

Let's Think About It

How are you intentionally discipling and training your child(ren) or young people in your sphere of influence?

_____

_____

_____

_____

_____

_____

_____

_____

_____

_____

_____

_____

_____

_____

_____

SALTY

Down to Earth Conversations

FAT DEMON'S COUSIN

*O*n Facebook, a friend of mind regularly refers to her struggles with weight with the hashtag #fatdemon. At times I reply to her with, "Fat Demon's cousin lives at my house." I have tried exorcising this demon with exercise, dieting, herbs, juicing, jazzercise, jogging (really fast walking), measuring, weighing, and a plethora of other remedies.

As a child, I was always a little larger than my classmates, but it really did not start bothering me until third grade when the kids started calling me Fat Mama. I can still remember the emotional pain of being the only one in my P.E. class who could not finish the allotted push-ups and sit-ups, and developing this terrible cramp in my stomach while trying to finish. I could never hang on the gym bars or do the flips that my friends did so effortlessly.

I have been called big boned, full-figured, healthy, chubby, and heavy-set. Since the age of 18, I have lost the same 20 pounds at least ten times. It does not help that I am the only overweight sibling; my sister and brother are both very thin like our parents. I remember being so envious of my siblings' physique and praying that I would become ill so I could lose weight. Unfortunately, the sadder I became, the more I ate. I have had every medical test and, no, I do not have an under-active thyroid or a slow metabolism; the truth is that I just love to eat high calorie foods and hate most physical exercise. I constantly compare myself to other overweight people, finding minimal comfort in that I am a little smaller than them.

Besides all of the stress and discouragement of gaining, losing, and gaining weight again can bring, it is also very distressing to notice how people furtively stare at me when I eat. I've stopped eating in public, feeling that people are secretly critiquing what and how much I'm eating. I also hate taking pictures with skinny people and looking at the pictures. You know the old adage "a picture is worth a 1000 words (and pounds)." I can put on my queen size leggings (over my spanks), my cute extra-large shirt and my plus size jacket and feel really cute until I see the picture, and pictures don't lie.

To say I hate my body would be an understatement. The reality is that I did not feel good about my body even when I was thinner. I can't remember a time when I was at peace with my weight.

Continuing the Conversation

Everyone has something they wish they could change about their physical appearance. How can we be confident in the skin God gave us and stop chasing that perfect body?

1. Love yourself exactly as you are, with all your physical attributes and challenges. You were made in God's image. (Genesis 1:27)

2. Free yourself from the concern of what people may think about you. Just pursue being pleasing to God. (Galatians 1:10)

3. View your body as a temple to be pleasing to God. Try to be healthy, not thin. (I Corinthians 6:19)

4. People come in different shapes and sizes. Make the most of the body that God gave you and focus on being beautiful on the inside, too. "People look at the outward appearance, but God looks at the heart." (I Samuel 16:7)

Let's Talk About It
Am I treating my body like a temple, pleasing to God? Do I focus on developing the inside of my temple or do I just prioritize my outward appearance?

_____

_____

_____

_____

_____

_____

_____

_____

_____

_____

_____

_____

WOULD YOU LOVE ME
IF YOU KNEW MY STORY?

I don't know if you would like me if you knew me.

What an odd thing to say, I thought. What is there to know? She looked well, flawless with her tailored suits, designer bags, beautiful hair, handsome husband, and thriving career. She controlled all the things that she could control. Her appearance always shined, but her smile, or the lack thereof, often betrayed her, telling the real story.

Still intrigued by her initial statement, I asked her if she wanted to join me for coffee on our next work break. She accepted the invitation, and soon we were seated in a corner of the breakroom with our steaming coffee mugs. After some casual conversation about the weather, I complimented her nice outfit, and that's when June started to confide in me about how she felt worthless and how her low self-esteem was destroying her life and that she felt completely hopeless.

June was raised by a single mom who was determined that her only child would have more than she had, socially and financially. Although her mom wanted the best for her daughter, her methods of achieving that were often brutal. June received little unconditional love as a child. She always had to be the best student, athlete, and daughter to receive affection or approval from her mother. Perfection was expected, and anything less was not accepted. June spent her childhood feeling inadequate and continually striving to be perfect to earn love.

As an adult, June constantly compared herself to others and felt she did not quite measure up. There was always someone else who was smarter, prettier, thinner, or richer than she was. She knew her thoughts were unhealthy and causing her to be stressed and depressed, but she couldn't seem to break out of the terrible mindset that she had been conditioned into her whole life. She had tried counselors and medication, and now she was seeking a friend – someone she could share her secret with. She felt she was always living a lie, and Louis Vuitton and Versace just weren't enough; they only helped for a fleeting moment, but the emptiness always returned.

Continuing the Conversation

Our self-worth is often measured by what people say about us. If the public reviews are favorable, we feel good about ourselves but if the commentary is marginal or poor, we are deflated; we feel that something is wrong with us.

Unfortunately, a lot of these feelings can stem from our childhood experiences. Let's examine where true self-worth comes from.

1. Often we feel that we are the only one with struggles, but the Bible states that rain falls on the just and unjust. No one escapes hardship in our world. (Matthew 5:45)

2. We have to remember that our worth comes from who we are in Christ Jesus. Houses, cars, careers, etc. are only temporal. (Romans 5:8)

3. Trust God to heal your emotions. God does still heal, emotionally and physically; seek professional and spiritual Christian counseling when needed. (Psalm 30:2, Psalm 147:3)

Let's Think About It

What insecurities are you living with? Whose standard are you trying to live up to?

_____

_____

_____

_____

_____

_____

_____

_____

_____

_____

_____

_____

_____

_____

THE CINDERELLA SYNDROME

Since my earliest memories, I wanted to be married. I think it all started when I first saw the Little Mermaid at 5 years old. I wanted to be Ariel and marry my prince charming. And I did marry the man of my dreams; my own personal Prince Charming. He was handsome, gifted, and a Christian. I enjoyed all of the little things he did for me, like taking out the trash, washing my car, and filling my car with gas.

When a few months passed and he told me to take out the trash, I just thought he was not feeling well. A week later, I told him that one of my car tires was low and he told me just to take care of it because he was too busy. He then casually added, "that was what they made Mike's Mechanic shop for." I knew he was having a hard time at his job and decided I didn't need to bother him further with such small details. Or, was I just making excuses?

I always looked forward to our regularly scheduled date nights. I loved spending time with him. Needless to say, I was disappointed when our weekly Friday night dates became monthly, then every other month, then almost non-existent. Finally, I was informed by Mr. Wonderful that we paid a lot of money for cable and did not need to go out any longer; we could just stay at home and watch Netflix movies and I could cook. (Finances were not an issue.)

We were always physically affectionate. Every morning on his way to work, he would kiss me good-bye. It would be hard for us to be in the same room without hugging or holding hands. So I was perplexed when he started walking past me without even a look my way. After only a year of marriage, I feel like I am living with a roommate; no dates, no hugging, no kissing, no affection. I want to be romanced, thought of, and loved, that's why I got married. I don't just want someone to share the bills with, or a roommate.

So what do I do? Do I fuss, nag, and fuss some more? Should I give him a piece of my mind? I rehearsed over and over what I wanted to tell him. Finally, I orchestrated the right time and words to share how I felt. Surely, when I shared how I felt, he would change back to Mr. Wonderful. He listened and said he would try. He tried for a while then returned to his selfish ways. I can't imagine spending another year with him and "'til death do us part" makes me want to jump off the roof. But what do I do?

Continuing the Conversation

After a few years of marriage, many women fall prey to the "Cinderella Syndrome," expecting their husband to court them like Prince Charming forever. These short-sighted wives ask the question, "What happened to my Knight in Shining Armor? How can I still love someone who is not showing me the love and affection I need?" Marriage is a long-term commitment, and men are wired differently than women. How can we, as wives, learn to show and receive love without any limitations?

1. Often we forget that the Christian life is a life of unconditional love and acceptance. Easy to say; hard to do consistently. To love like Christ does require a daily dying to oneself. It's not looking out for yourself only, but also the needs of others (Phil 2:4). Especially our husbands, even if and when we feel that they don't deserve it. In fact, we need to love harder and deeper when we feel someone does not deserve it. Have you ever told God that it is ok if you don't get all of the affection and attention you crave? No human loves perfectly, but often we put demands on others to do so. Your mate is not perfect, and neither are you. The Bible says that all have sinned (Romans 3:23), and knights in shining armor are only in fairy tales. (I Corinthians 13)

2. Consider modeling the type of love and affection you want so desperately from your husband. The Bible says that though we were hostile towards Christ, yet He still loved us. (Romans 5:10) To be really Christ-like, we have to learn to love the unlovely. Do we love our mates like that? Daily, pray for your husband and seek to give the love that you want. Many men have not had godly role models. Some men have been told not to show emotions or affection. And yes, men have insecurities and can be afraid of rejection or appearing weak. Men need affirmation, too, and sometimes they have to be taught how to show affection. Dig deep and start by showing respect and affection to your husband every day, even if you don't feel like it, and eventually your feelings will follow your actions. (Ephesians 4:2)

3. No husband can fulfill his wife's every need. Find other appropriate avenues for fulfillment. Get active in a ministry. Seek out opportunities for community service. Enjoy life with girlfriends and extended family. Find your ultimate fulfillment in Christ. (Psalm 37:4)

Let's Think About It

Do I love my husband unconditionally? Am I honoring and respecting my husband?

_____

_____

_____

_____

_____

_____

_____

_____

_____

_____

_____

_____

_____

_____

_____

My Mother's Keeper

$\mathcal{W}$hy do I know how a single mom feels? I was 21 with two babies, ages one and three, and it was obvious that I was married to a person who was not emotionally or financially ready to be a husband or father. I took fifteen dollars and left Chicago on a Greyhound bus traveling back home. I came home comforted in knowing that I could stay for a while with my mom and step dad until I got on my feet. To my surprise, I was informed by my mother one evening at 10pm that I could only stay there one more night because my step dad wanted to rent out the room.

I was so afraid, with nowhere to turn. How was I going to take care of my babies? How could my step dad be so cruel? How could my mom let him do this? I stayed up all night praying and wondering what I was going to do, where I was going to turn. By 8am the next morning, God impressed upon me to go and talk to an elderly neighbor, Ms. Davis.

I asked Ms. Davis if she would keep my babies for

two months to give me a chance to get a job and find a place to live. To my surprise, she said yes. I immediately left the babies with Ms. Davis, moved in with a girlfriend, and began my search for a job.

Two months later, I had two jobs, an apartment, and my babies back. Ms. Davis continued to babysit my girls while I worked. I was so young and naïve, I didn't even know that I could have received public assistance, but Ms. Davis was my public assistance. God sent another angel in the form of the girls' paternal grandmother. Faithfully, for fifteen years, on the first of the month, she would send me $20.00 with a little note attached that read "for the girls." I usually used all of the money from both of my jobs to pay the rent and utilities; often that $20.00 would feed us for the month.

I knew that this road would not be easy, but I was committed to raising my two daughters to the best of my ability. The next eighteen years were full of lean meals, second-hand clothes, juggling bills, and sacrifice. It was my deepest desire that my girls would receive a good education and live a full life. Every day, I woke up with this goal on my mind. That goal and my faith gave me the strength to continue my journey.

Continuing the Conversation

Life is not always a rose garden. Most single parents don't wake up one morning planning to become single parents, but because we live in a fallen world, it happens. How can we encourage single parents in our communities?

1. Don't be judgmental. Love them where they are, unconditionally. The events that lead to their current situation are varied and sometimes complex. Remember, "but by the grace of God go I." You could be in the same situation if it had not been for God's goodness and protection in your life. (John 8:7, Matthew 7:1-5)

2. Be open to ways that you can minister to single-parent families. God often will bring a need to your attention. Remain sensitive to the Holy Spirit's leading in ways you can assist. Because most single parents live on limited incomes, financial gifts are always nice, but acts of service are also welcomed. Childcare, car repair, or yard work can really bless a family. Think about including a single-parent family in your holiday celebration. You can also demonstrate the love of Christ by just being a friend, offering a listening ear and prayer, and giving encouragement. (I Peter 4:10, Luke 6:38)

Let's Think About It

How can I serve a single-parent family or someone in need this year?

_____

_____

_____

_____

_____

_____

_____

_____

_____

_____

_____

_____

_____

LOST

*N*othing prepares you for the loss of someone you love. Everyone tells you to rejoice because your loved one is in heaven. But no one tells you how to cope when you wake up with them on your mind or how to do life without them. What do you do when you hear their favorite song and you want to sing it with them or just share a silly moment and laugh with them?

Moving on with life without that loved one; especially a parent is one of the hardest trials in life to conquer. A mother and child relationship is always that, even if the child is an adult. When that bond is broken by death, that grown child has a very difficult time moving forward, because mom has been a faithful staple in your life.

My mom passed away shortly after the birth of my second child. My daughter was 4 years old and my son was 6 months old. As I had struggled with postpartum depression after the birth of my son, I realized the sudden death of my mom caused me to slip into a state of emptiness, despair, and confusion. I lived in a fog for three months, not knowing how to function well; I desperately wanted and needed my mom to share in the new milestones I was encountering daily.

The reality of her death didn't set in immediately, but gradually. When we cleaned out her closets, in my grief, I chose to keep so many pieces that had valuable memories to me; the dress she wore in my wedding, the apron she always cooked in, her favorite broomstick skirts. I took some of her clothing and wore them from time to time, even though they all just hung on me. I felt as though these things kept her close to me.

When my daughter's preschool announced plans for "Grandparents' Day," it hit me like a brick. I realized, through a flood of tears, that my daughter no longer had a grandmother (of course my husband's parents were available, but no one could take the place of my mother). Within a few months, my daughter lost her first tooth. I wanted to ask her, "Mom, what do I do?" I sat holding my daughter and the telephone, realizing there was nothing to do, but I needed her to tell me that.

My coping was not going very well. I remember keeping the last voice mail she left me for about two years, her hand written recipes became my prized possessions, and I regularly told my siblings, "You know what mama would say." These were all ways that helped her to live on with me during the days of grief. And even today, so many years later, I pride myself on remembering the lessons she gave me about education, character and serving my family.

After a year, I was still encountering meltdowns that often interfered with my daily responsibilities, so I eventually sought Christian counseling for my grief and was given a new perspective. I accepted the cycle of life, celebrated the victories we experienced together, and also learned to let go of regrets.

As I sought healing, I asked God to give me peace and understanding with the assurance that this, too, was His plan. I knew if I would trust Him to provide for me through adversity, he would show me that he was in control of my life and my mom was His. God has been faithful to bring surrogate grandparents for my children, women of wisdom to speak to me, and I now have a heart to comfort those who experience loss and share God's strength with them. (II Corinthians 1:3-5)

Continuing the Conversation

What I experienced was not just a trial, but an opportunity to grow closer to God and reflect on how my mom celebrated life with me. My new perspective helped me to understand those blessings and the new life my mom received on the other side, not just the pain I had on this side.

1. Ecclesiastes 3:2 tells us that there is a time to be born and a time to die, but sometimes we have difficulty understanding this truth. However, to move forward, we must accept it.

2. Experiencing adversity makes us realize we are not in control of our lives. God's unchangeable hand has given us the blessing and the loss. Often, we have to make a deliberate decision to trust God. I knew no other path but to spend time with the Lord. (Psalm 119:71, Romans 8:18)

3. When grief or any situation seems to consume your life, God's word encourages us to seek godly counsel; it's okay to ask for help, your loved one would not want your life to be halted. (Proverbs 1:5, Proverbs 19:20)

Let's Think About It

You can grieve the loss of a person, thing, or dream. How has grief impacted your life?

_____

_____

_____

_____

_____

_____

_____

_____

_____

_____

_____

_____

_____

_____

_____

_____

TOTALLY COMMITTED

Hey Sweet,

I love when I get the opportunity to brag on you and how you've been the perfect mate for me. Does that make you perfect? No, and that's great, because two broken, imperfect people connected so many years ago and decided that a covenant relationship is what we would strive for, even if we didn't have a clue as to what that meant. I'm often asked what makes this relationship work, and yes, I could come up with some flippant answer like, "he's my best friend"... but if the truth were known, some days I choose to say "yes" when my heart says "no." There are days when my best friend is NOT you. I have made the hard choice to honor our covenant and vows and to work at this union as hard as I can. I'm totally committed even on the days when I don't like you, to respect and honor you in a way that models a godly marriage so our Heavenly Father will be pleased.

Thank you for loving me when the baggage of my life (insecurities, past hurts, and regrets) was packed so neatly into compartments that it made your head swim. "God don't waste nothing." He is able to look right through all of our mess and see the Christ in us. It is only because of Christ that for 26 years you have been my confidant, my friend, my go-to, my sounding board. You have allowed me to be me. You have trusted me with your heart, your health, our children, the management of our home, and the privilege to speak truth to you even when you didn't want to hear it. Thank you for being the godly man who has loved me even when I am hard to love.

Always,
K.

Continuing the Conversation

Marriage is hard work, and we need to approach it like we do that valued job. At our workplace, we want a good appraisal, approval and high marks. We want to receive a "well done" and give our best daily. We should strive to work even harder for our marriages.

1. Choosing to love someone is a decision. Even believers live in imperfect bodies and are prone to selfishness. Commitment is loving someone through the ups and downs of life, whether we feel like it or not. (I Peter 4:8)

2. Communication is the key to all healthy marriages. The Bible tells us to speak the truth in love. Keep your intonation and body language positive even when discussing serious issues. Be a good listener, trying to understand what your mate is saying instead of defending your point. (Ephesians 4:29, Ephesians 4:15)

Let's Talk About It

Am I speaking the truth in love? Am I choosing daily to love my mate and family?

_____

_____

_____

_____

_____

_____

_____

_____

_____

_____

_____

_____

_____

_____

_____

_____

ABOUT THE AUTHORS

Dr. Shailendra Thomas has served in Christian ministry for three decades, serving as women's and children's ministry leader, Bible study teacher, and seminar speaker. Dr. Thomas's experience in education extends over 30 years, serving as an elementary school teacher, instructional specialist, educational consultant, adjunct college professor, Principal at Fellowship Christian Academy and National Accreditation Commissioner for the Association of Christian Schools International.

Dr. Thomas enjoys serving and encouraging women by teaching Biblical truths. She led the women's ministry at Oak Cliff Bible Fellowship for several years and was instrumental in the development of discipleship programs, retreats, and bible studies for women. She has ministered to women of various cultures and denominations on topics, such as, marriage, parenting, and spiritual growth at conferences and seminars throughout the Dallas metroplex.

Dr. Thomas currently serves as Head of School at Scofield Christian School; however, her primary ministry is to her husband of 36 years, Richard, three grown daughters, Lorren, Hillary, and Chelsea, and one grandson, Landon Blake.

Marilyn Randle is absolutely in love with words. A Texas native, her inspiration comes daily through her roles as a wife, mother, daughter, sister, aunt and friend, as well as through deep affection for her hometown of Fort Worth.

In 1982, after living on both coasts, she married her husband Gary and returned to Texas to start a family. For more than two decades, she and Gary have partnered in ministry. They have one adult daughter, Gabrielle.

Marilyn is passionate about travel and has spent most of her adult life seeing the world. She is equally passionate about mentoring. She considers it a privilege to be able to speak into the lives of women. And if hospitality is a hallmark of southern living, then Marilyn just might be the gold standard. To her, it's second nature. To friends, a comfortable afternoon spent at her Arlington home is a rich experience, like getting a beautifully wrapped gift box filled with great memories and new traditions to take with you and enjoy for a lifetime.

Jennifer Smith is the consummate Christian professional educator, serving the past 20 years in public and private school systems. She earned a bachelor's degree from University of Texas at Arlington and a Master's degree in Education from Indiana Wesleyan University. Jennifer is known as a teacher who is passionate about educating the *whole child* and will not rest until all of her students experience success.

Real and down to earth are often terms used to describe Jennifer. She is very relational and is known for her many friendships at work, church, and in her community. She enjoys staying fit and can often be found jogging in the neighborhood. She resides in DeSoto, Texas, a small suburb of Dallas, where she and her husband Doug are raising three children, Tyler, Douglass, and Clarissa.

CONTACT THE AUTHORS

Do you have a coveted conversation that you would like to share?

Email your story to
friends@covetedconversations.com.

Want to become a part of a dynamic on-line women's support group where women are encouraged, inspired, and refreshed?

Go to
facebook.com/covetedconversations
and join the group.

Want to help others? A percentage of all proceeds from the book sales will be donated to a ministry that supports single mothers.

Read more Coveted Conversations at
www.covetedconversations.com